THIS BOOK

BELONGS TO:

- - - - - - - - - - - - - - -

- - - - - - - - - - - - - - -

- - - - - - - - - - - - - - -

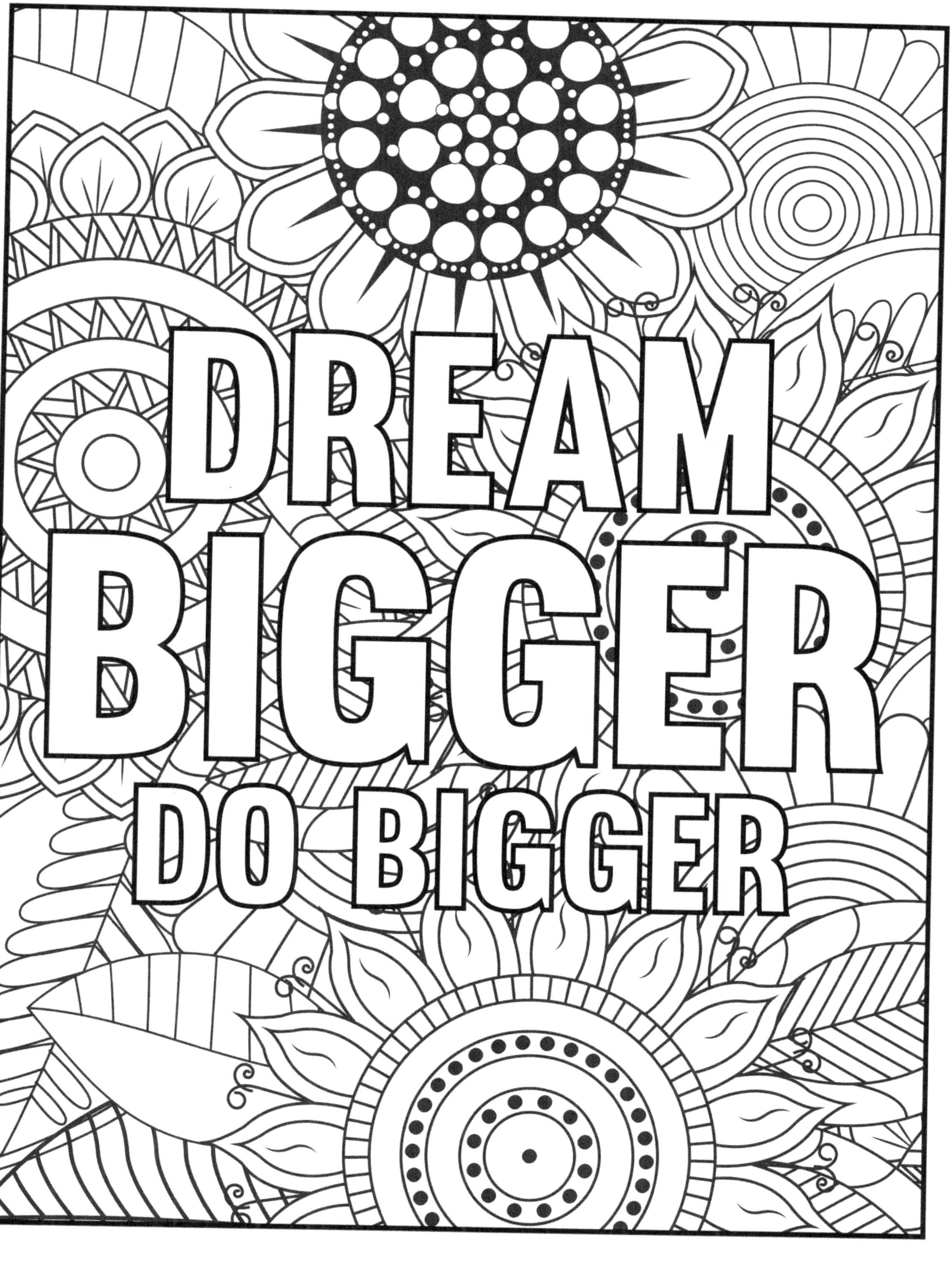
DREAM
BIGGER
DO BIGGER

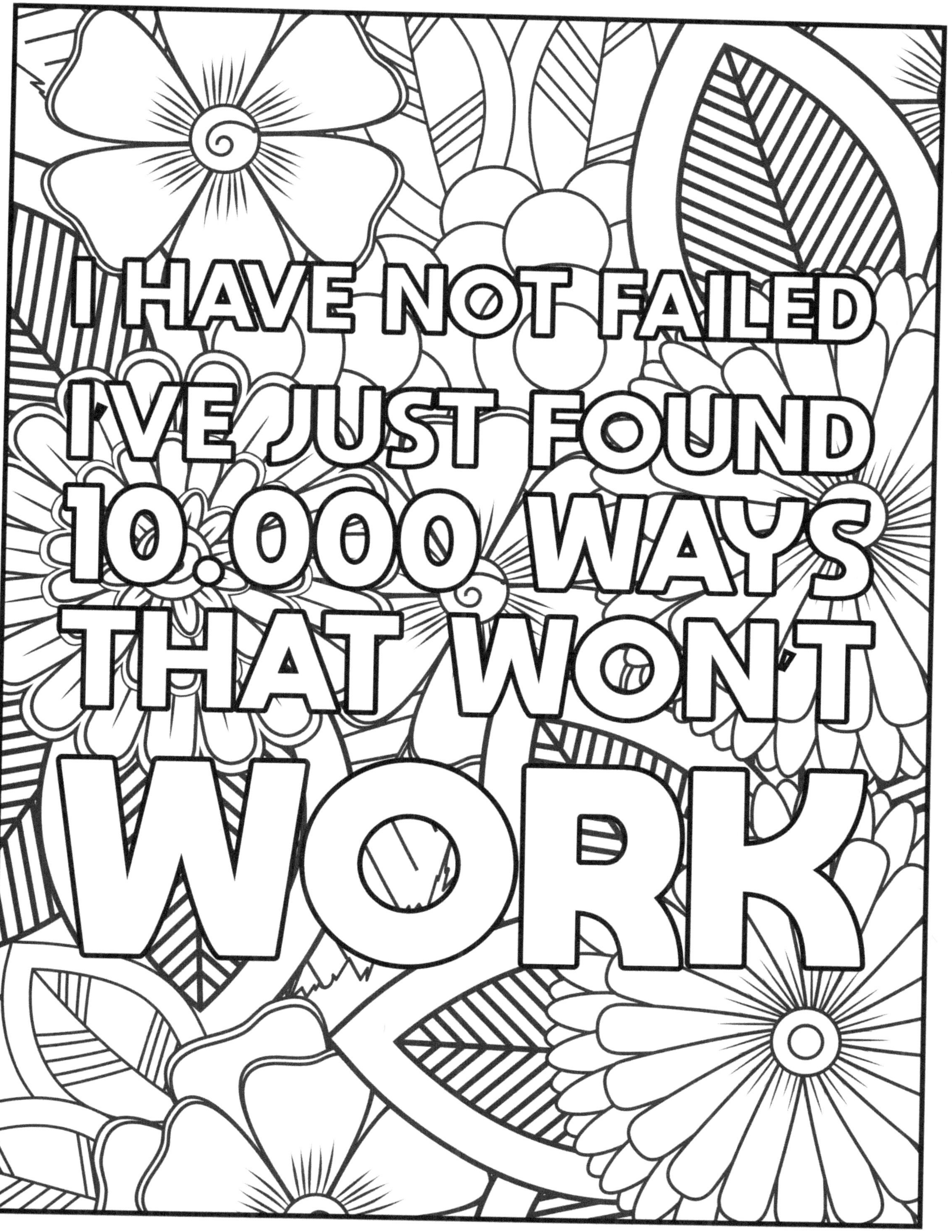
I HAVE NOT FAILED
I'VE JUST FOUND
10.000 WAYS
THAT WON'T
WORK

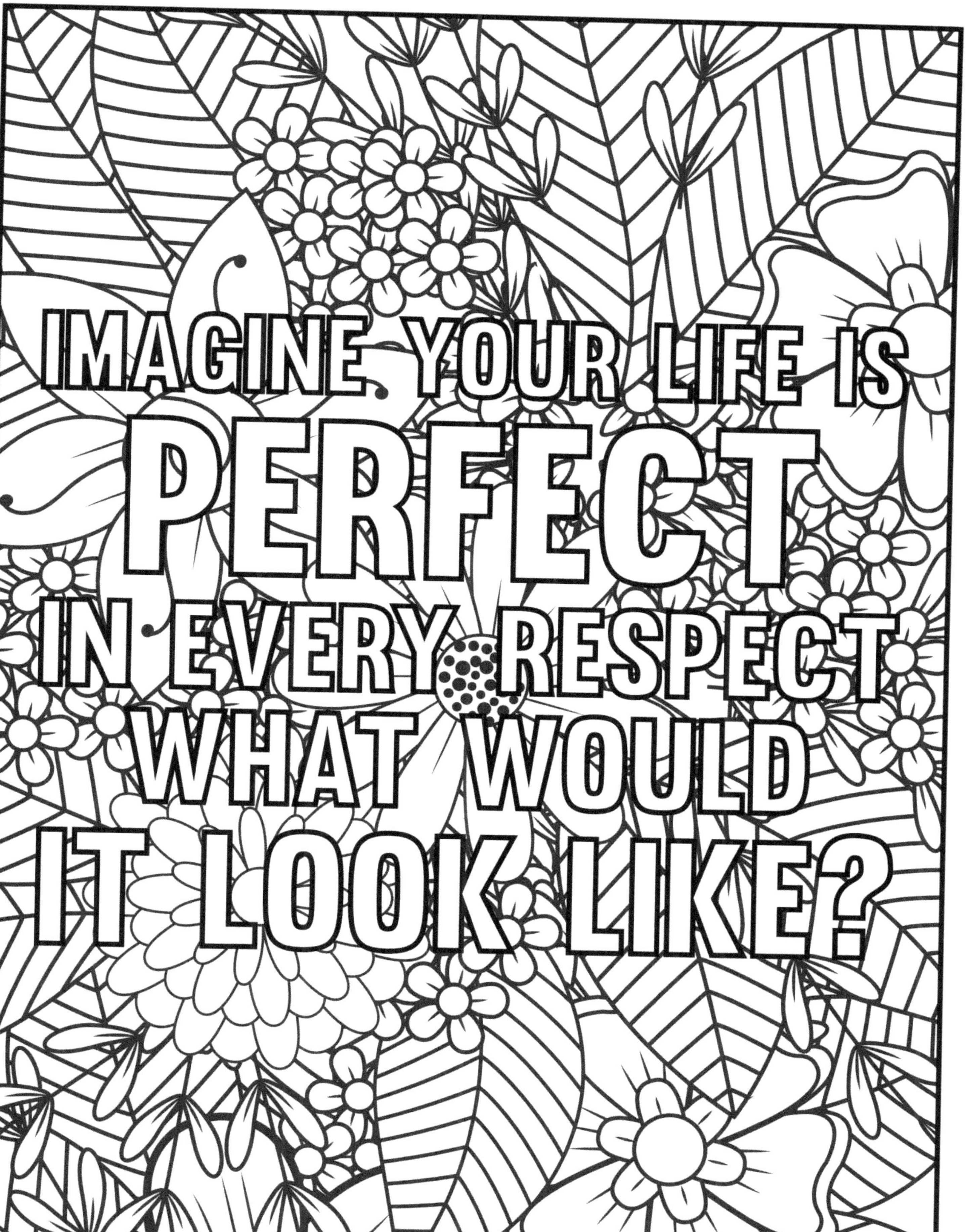
IMAGINE YOUR LIFE IS
PERFECT
IN EVERY RESPECT
WHAT WOULD
IT LOOK LIKE?

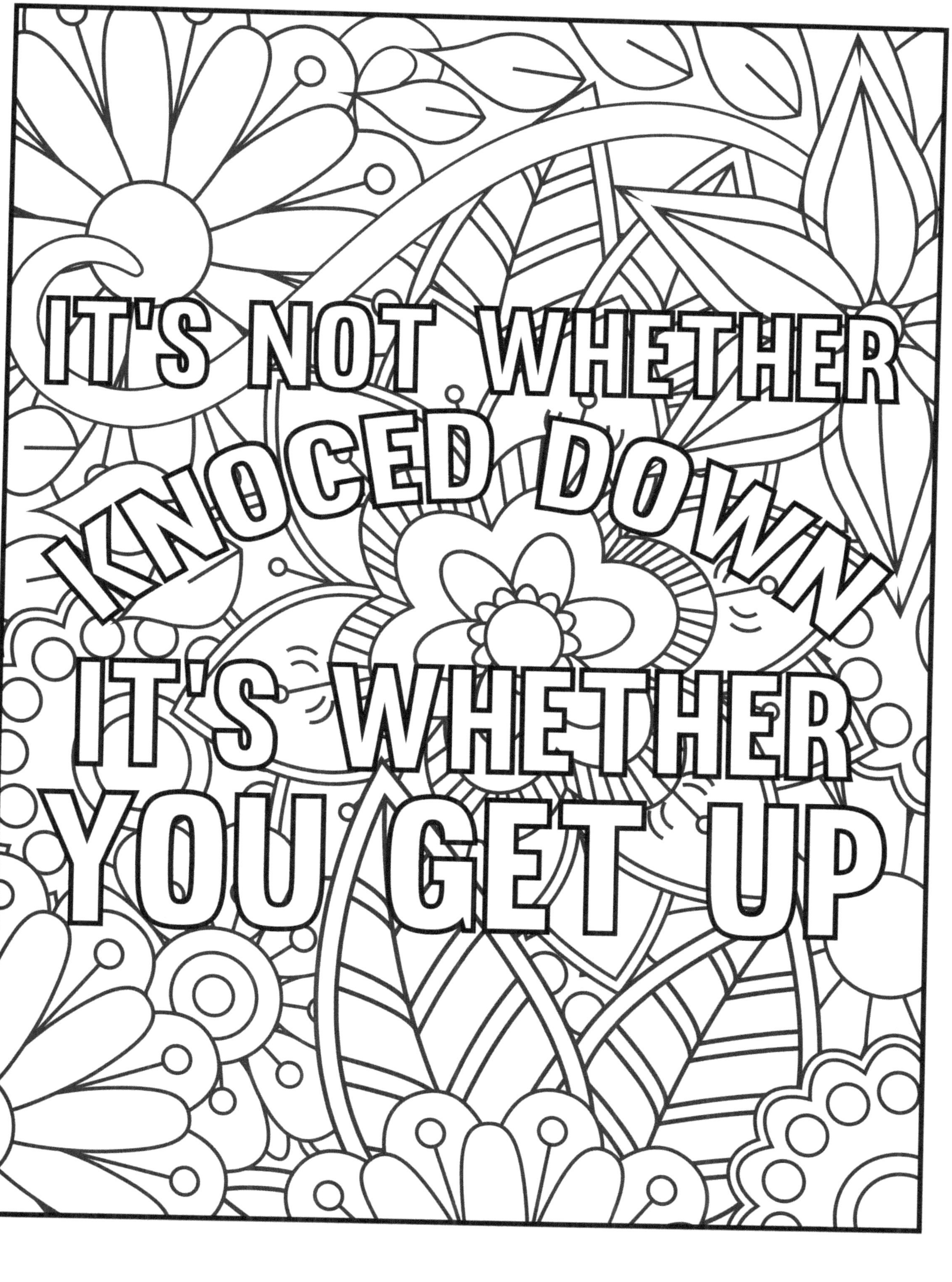
IT'S NOT WHETHER
KNOCED DOWN
IT'S WHETHER
YOU GET UP

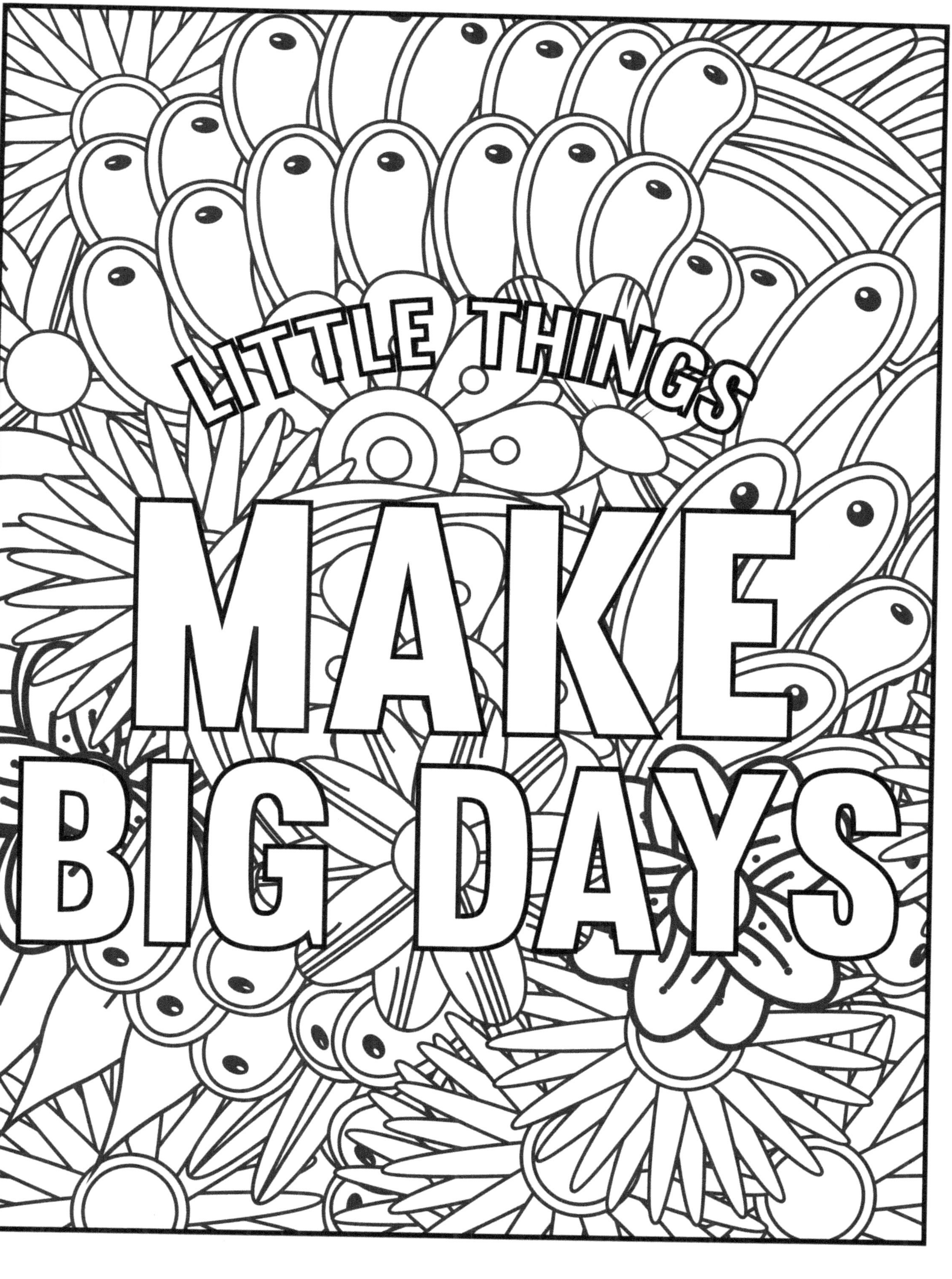
LITTLE THINGS
MAKE
BIG DAYS

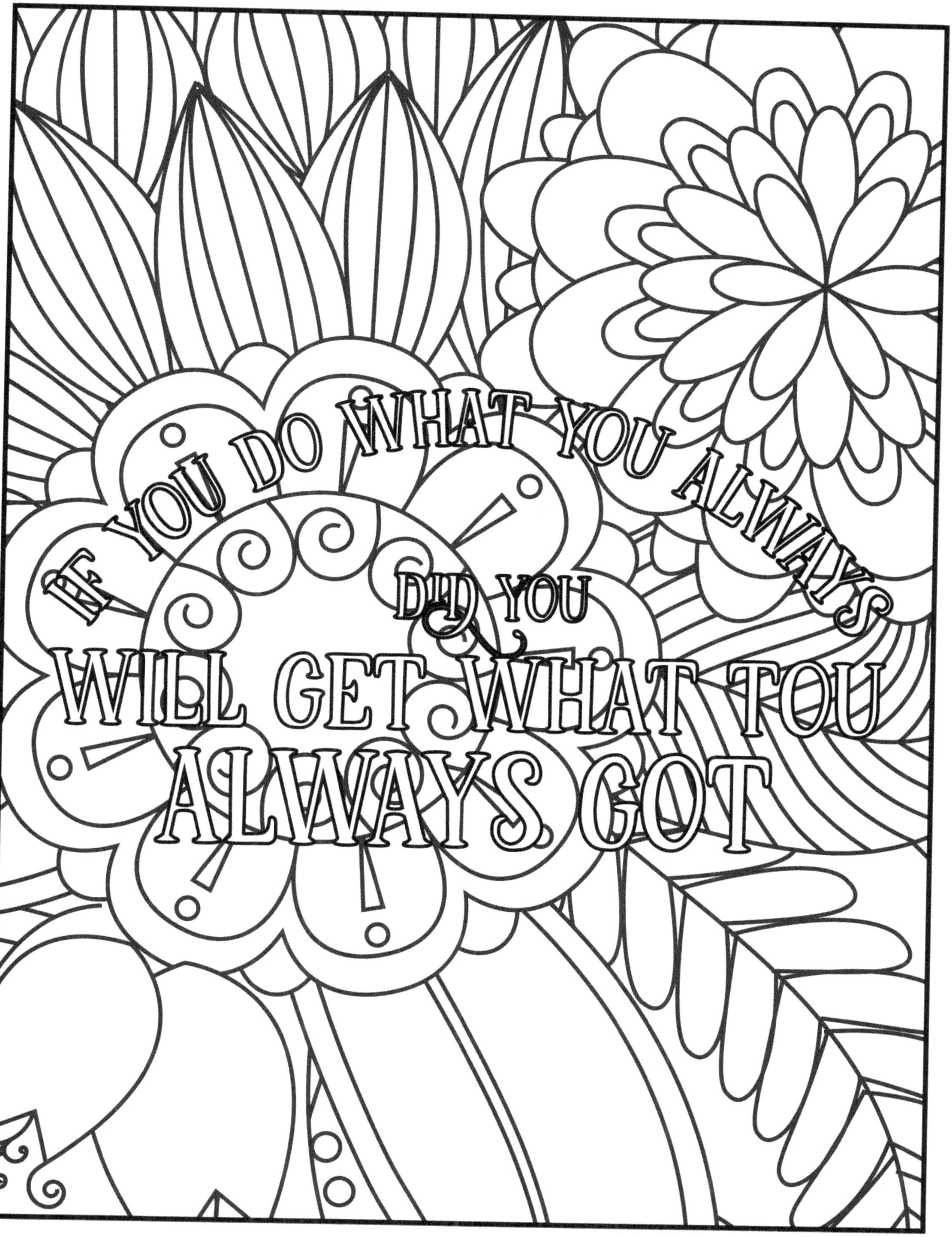
IF YOU DO WHAT YOU ALWAYS
DID YOU
WILL GET WHAT TOU
ALWAYS GOT

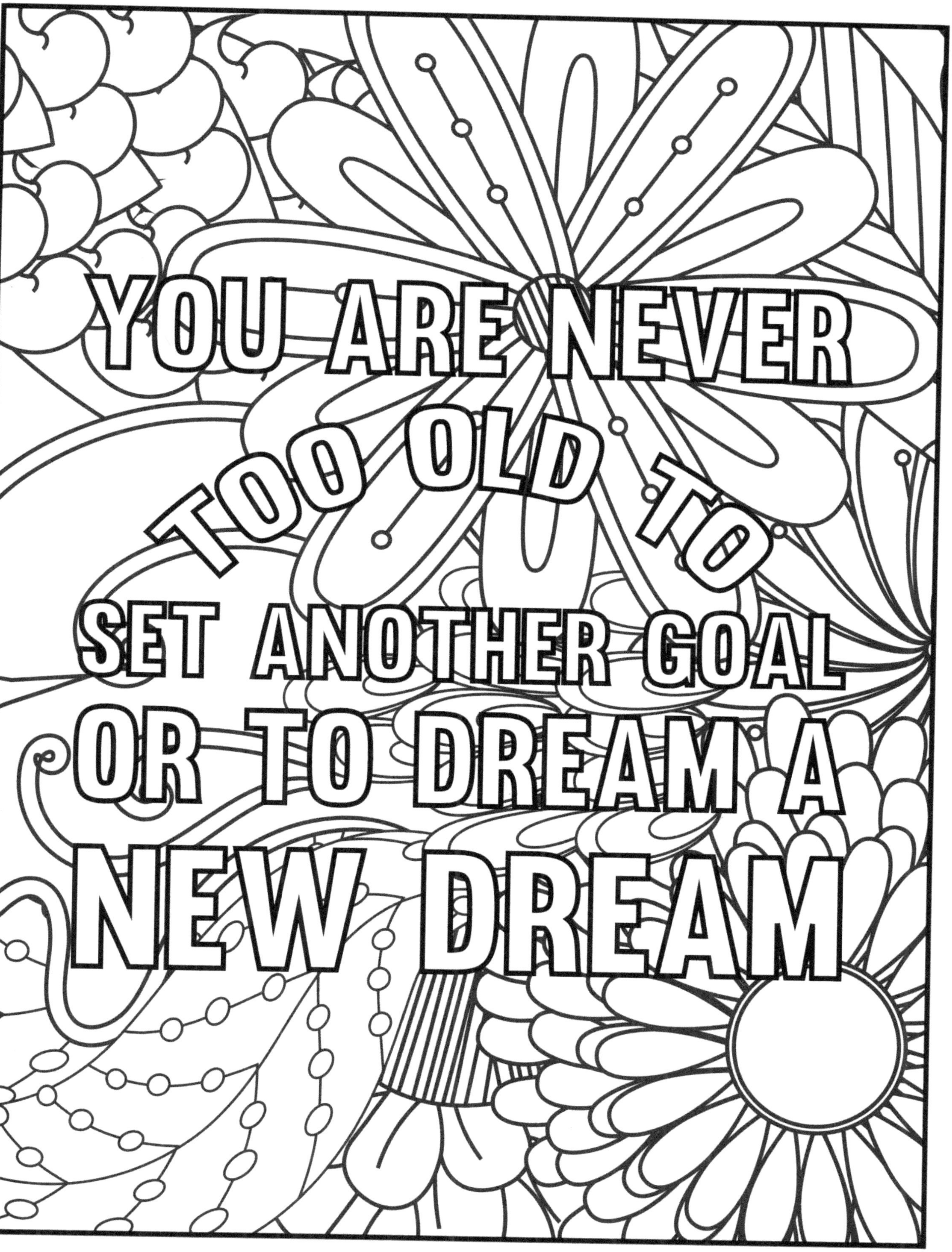
YOU ARE NEVER
TOO OLD TO
SET ANOTHER GOAL
OR TO DREAM A
NEW DREAM

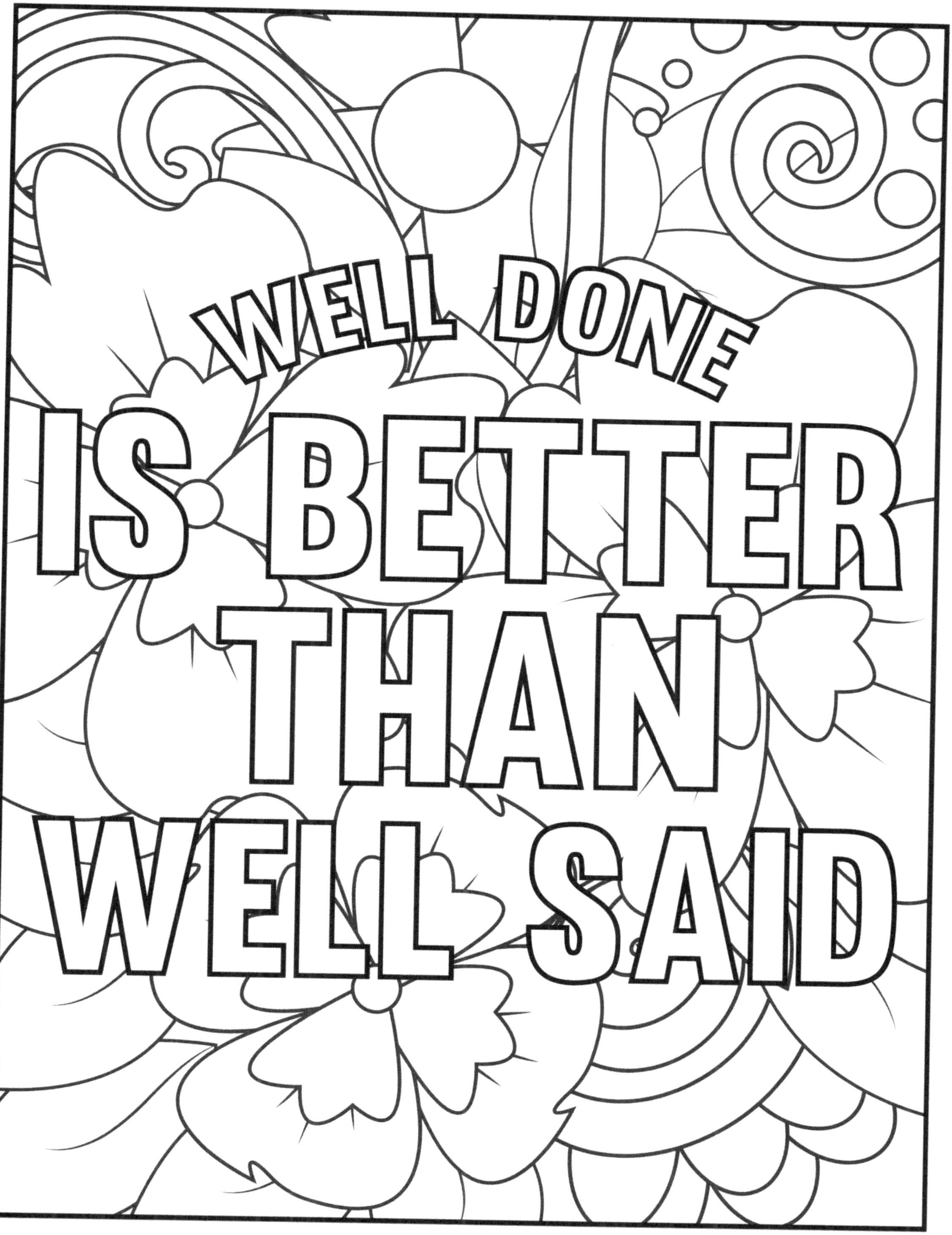
WELL DONE
IS BETTER
THAN
WELL SAID

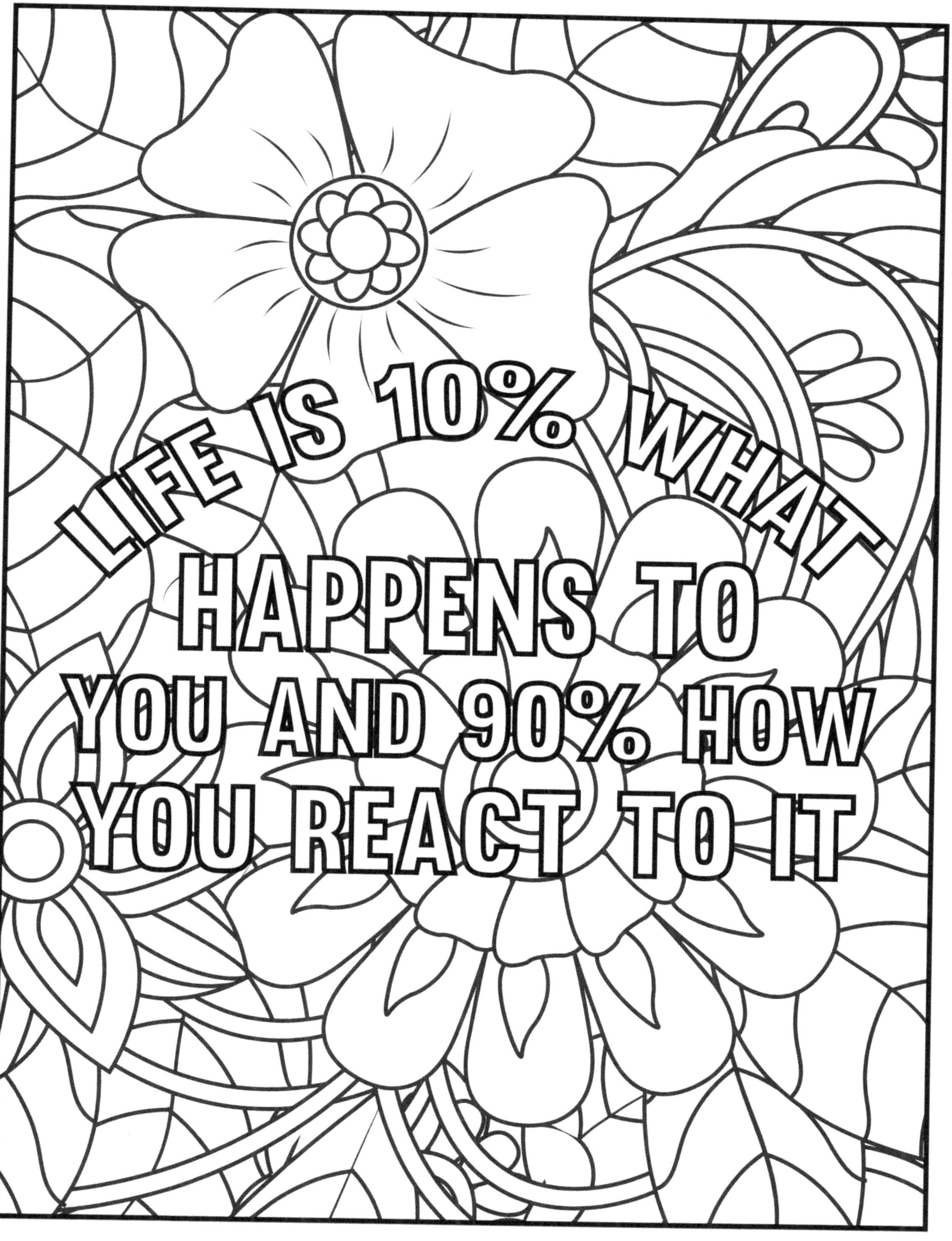
LIFE IS 10% WHAT
HAPPENS TO
YOU AND 90% HOW
YOU REACT TO IT

THE SECRET
OF GETTING
AHEAD IS
GETTING STARTED

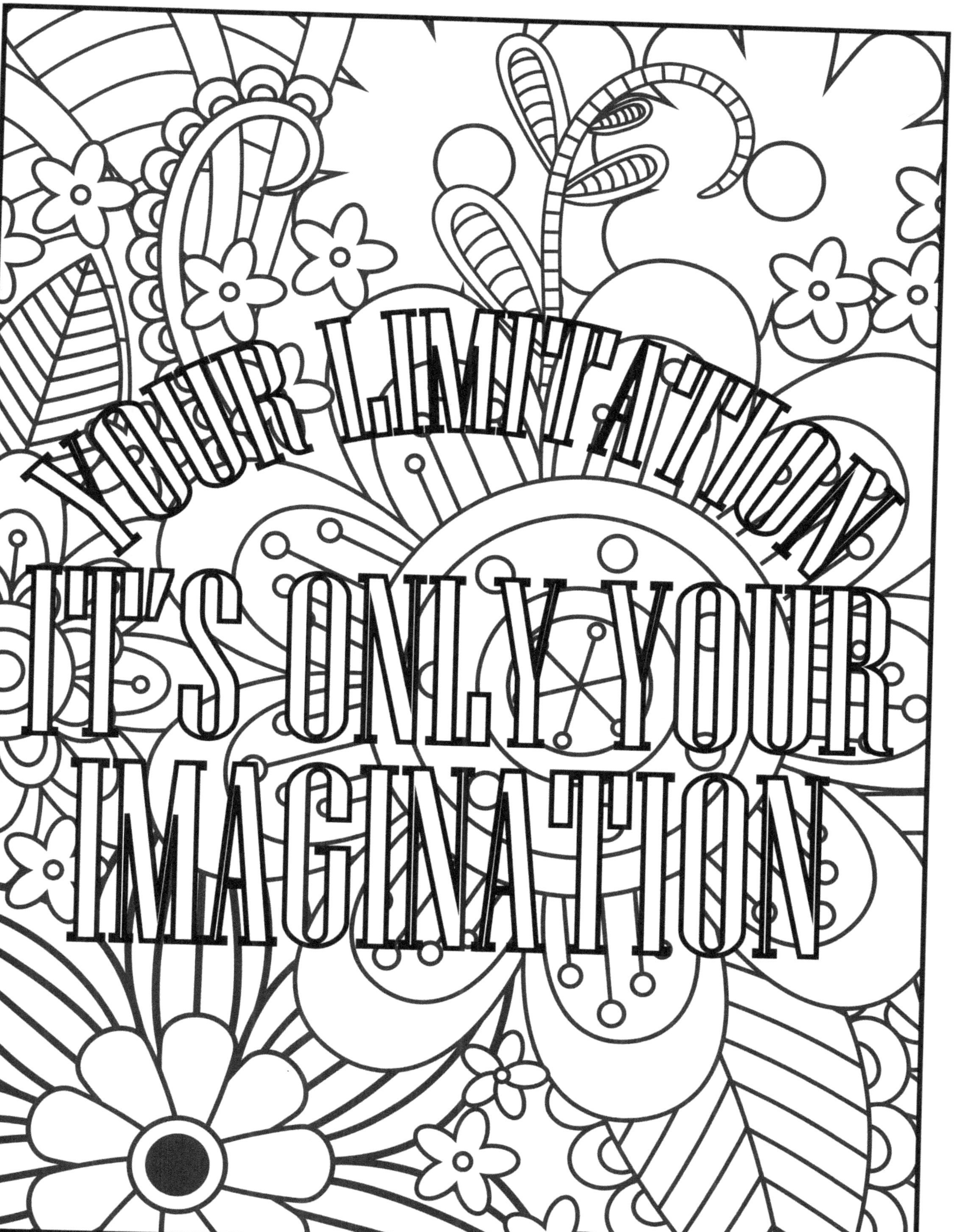
YOUR LIMITATION
IT'S ONLY YOUR
IMAGINATION

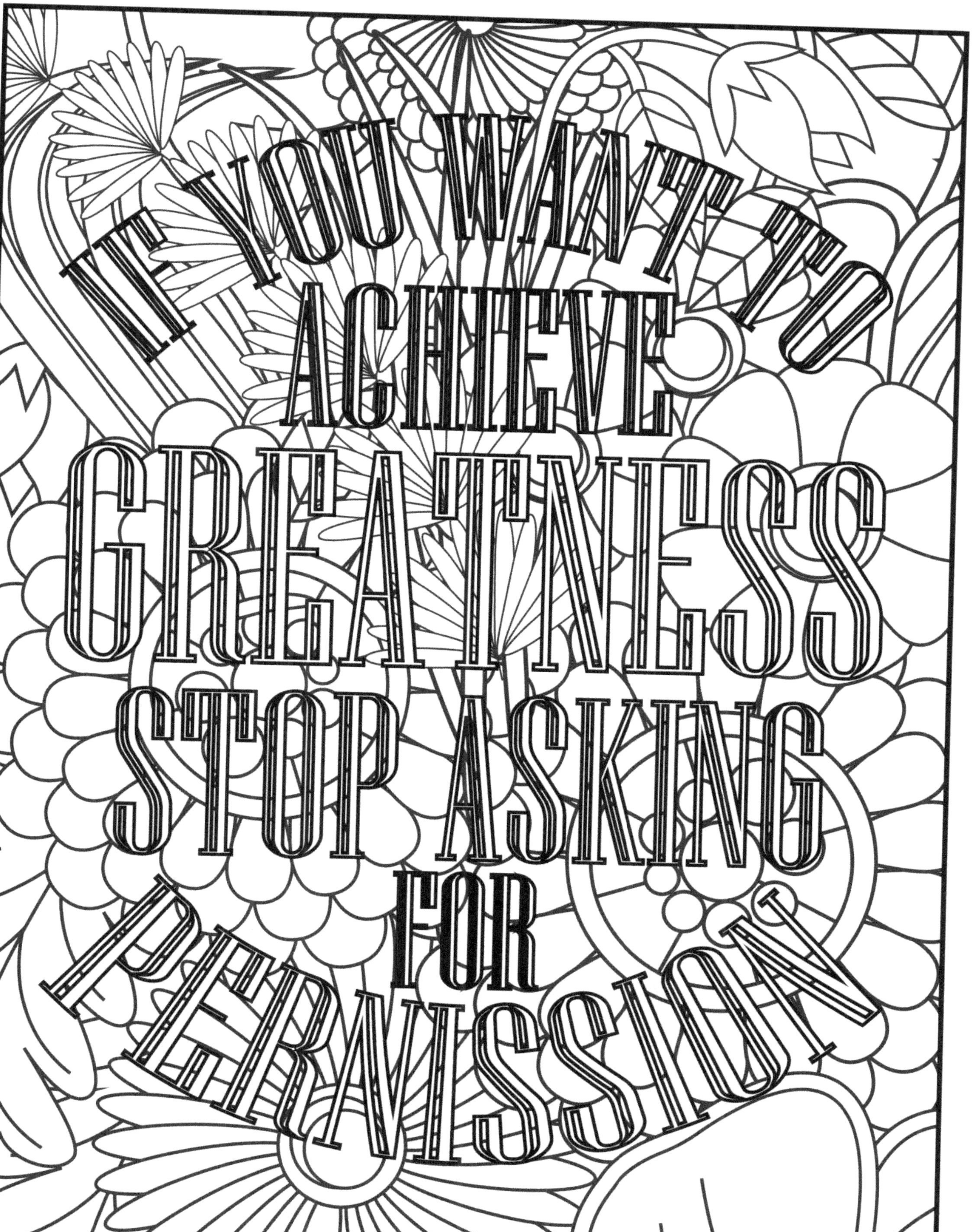
IF YOU WANT TO
ACHIEVE
GREATNESS
STOP ASKING
FOR
PERMISSION

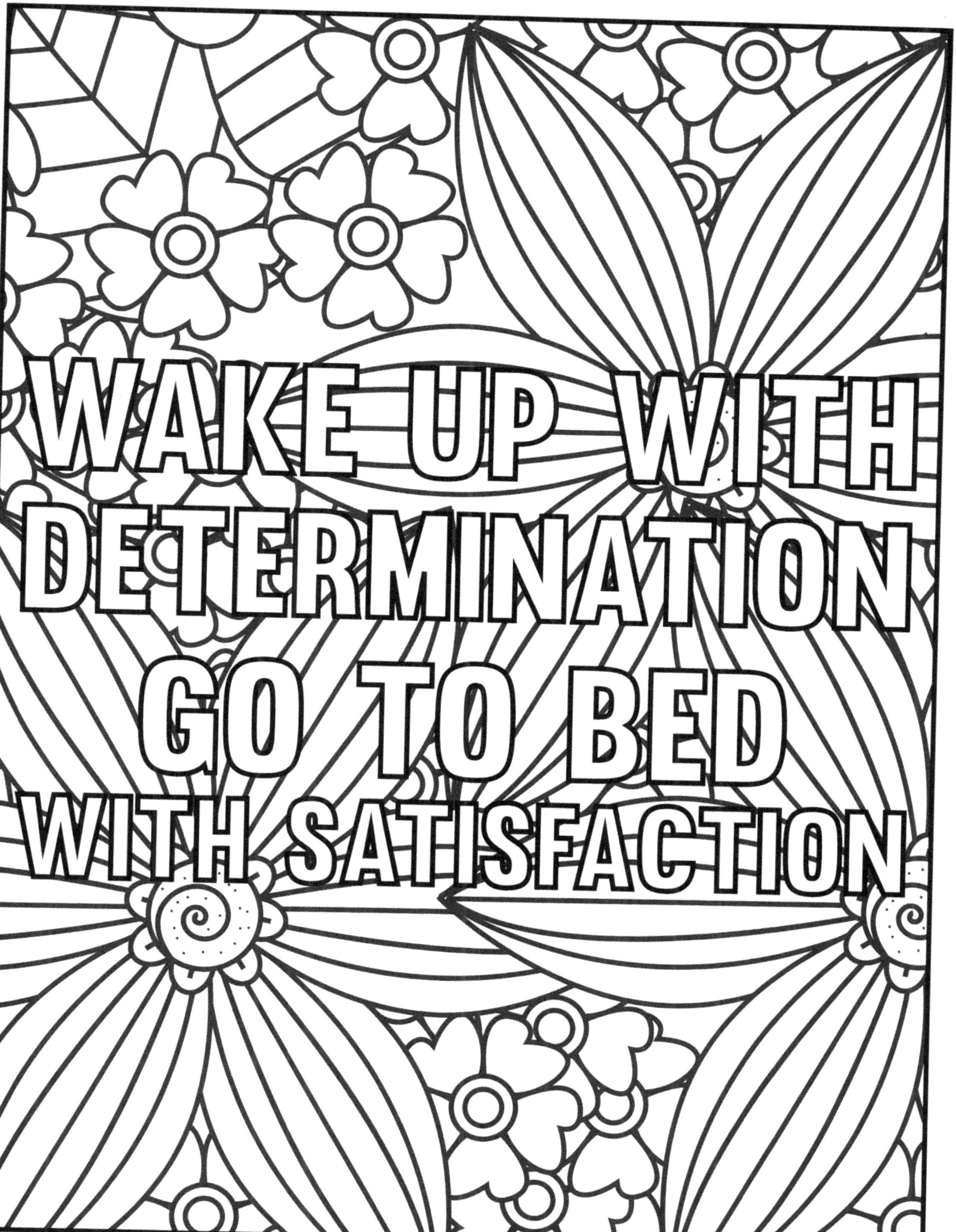
WAKE UP WITH
DETERMINATION
GO TO BED
WITH SATISFACTION

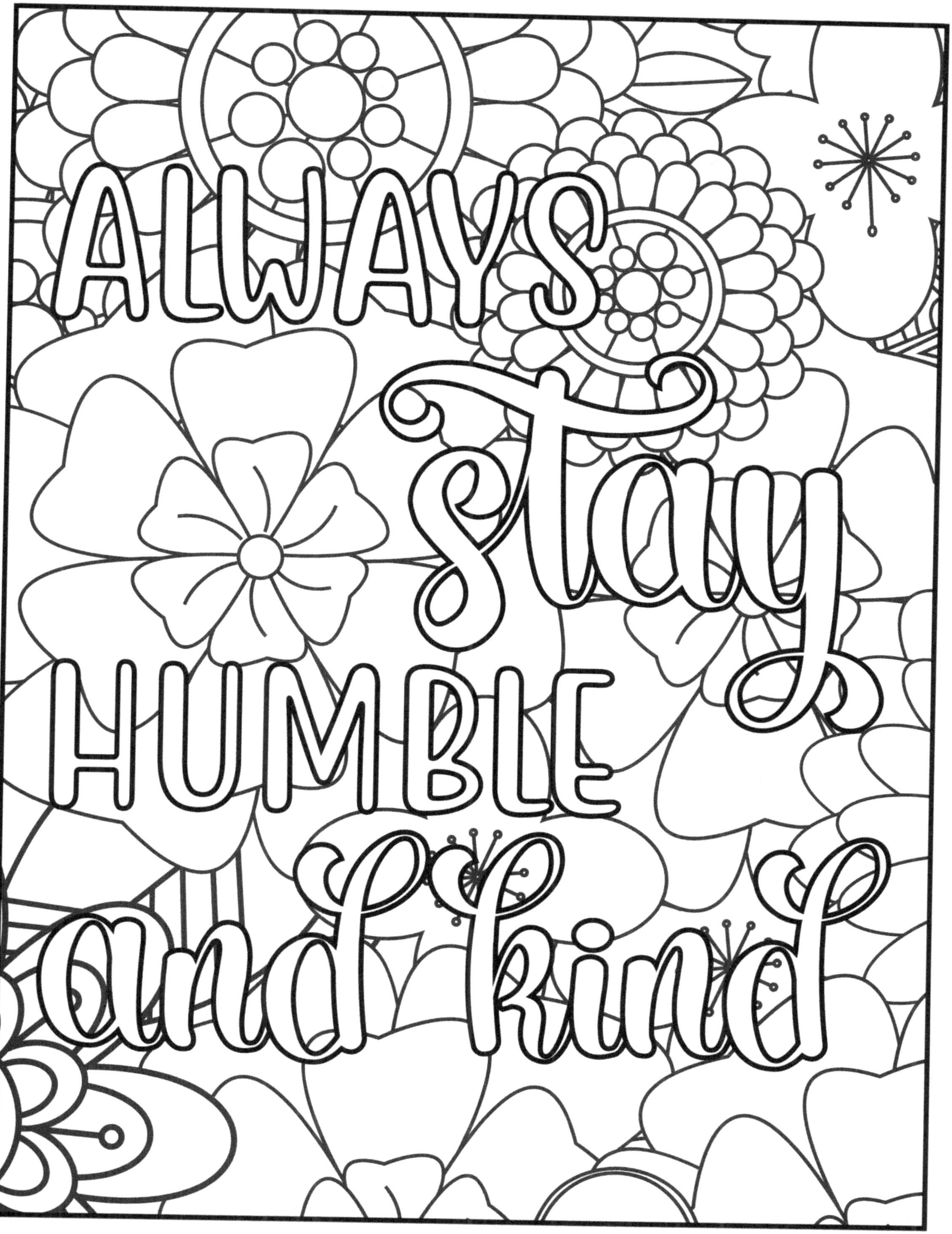
ALWAYS
Stay
HUMBLE
and kind

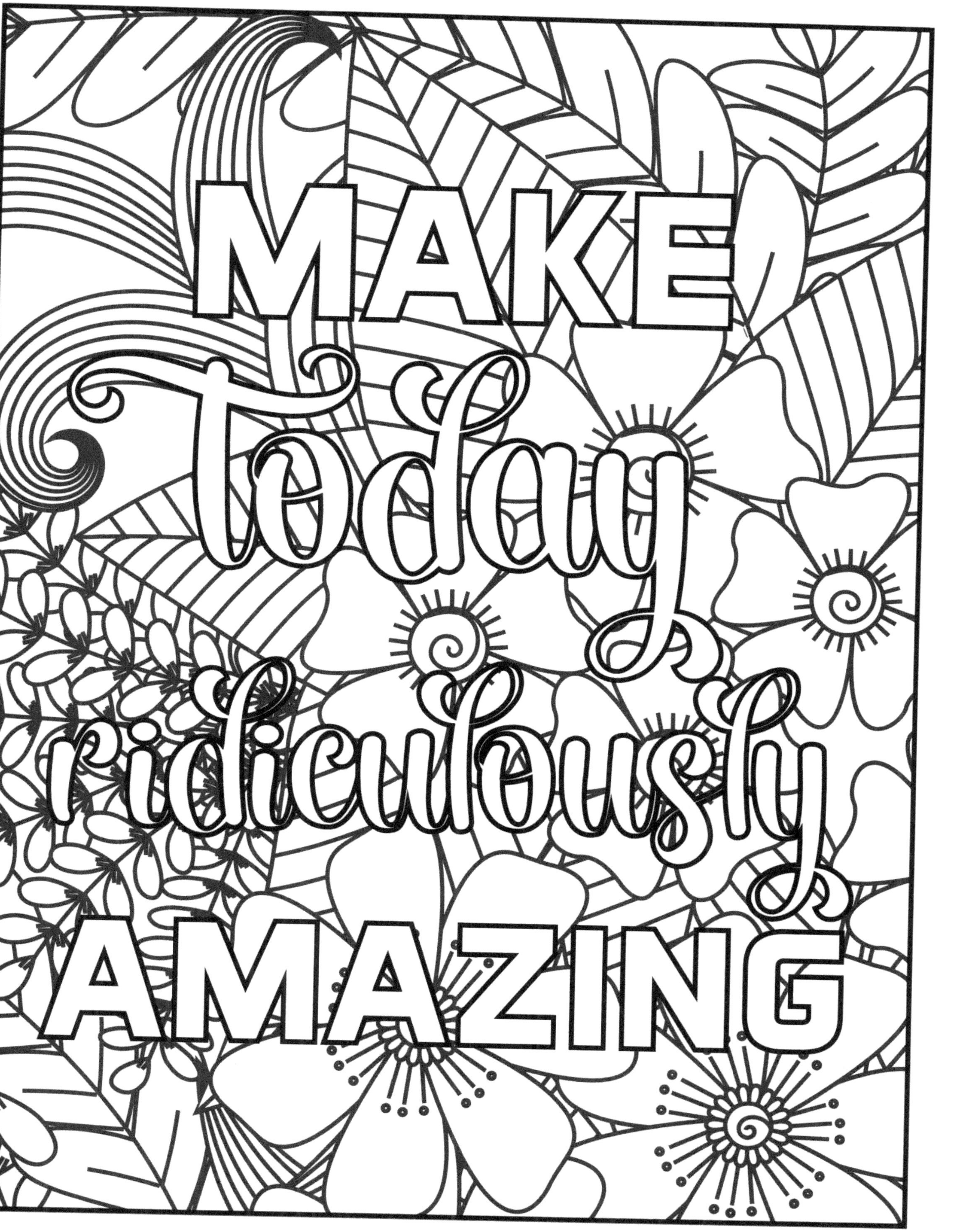
MAKE
today
ridiculously
AMAZING

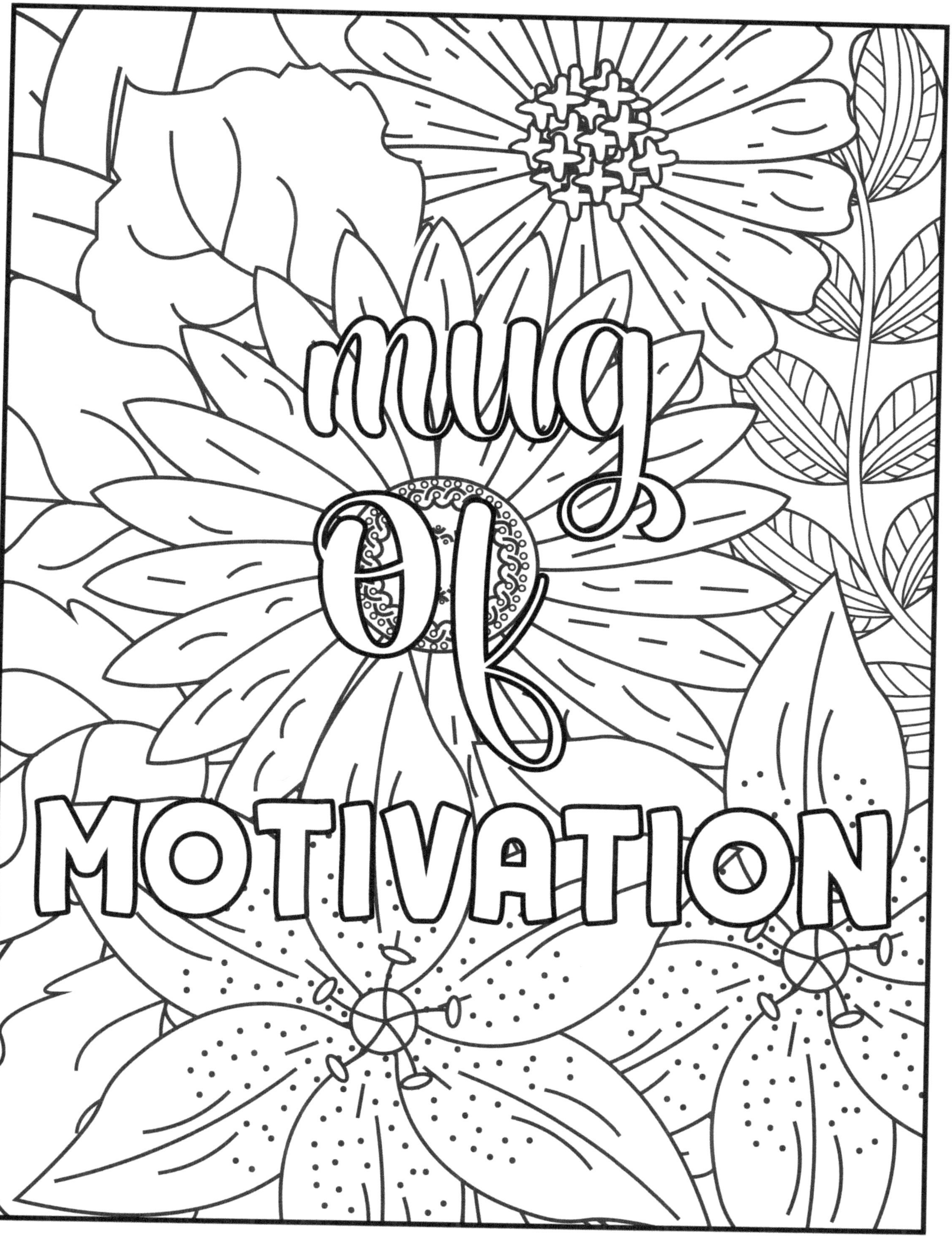
mug
of
MOTIVATION

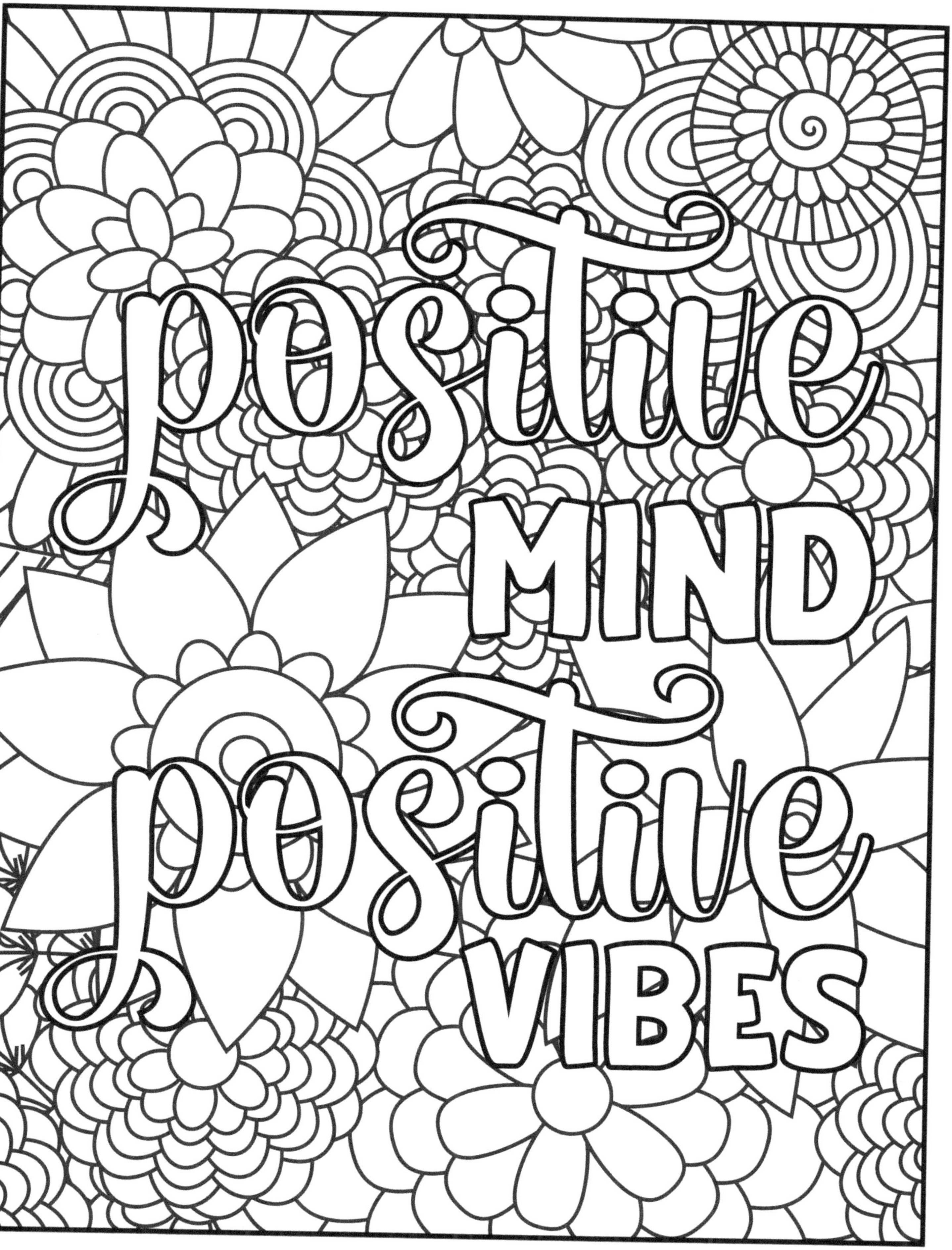
positive
MIND
positive
VIBES

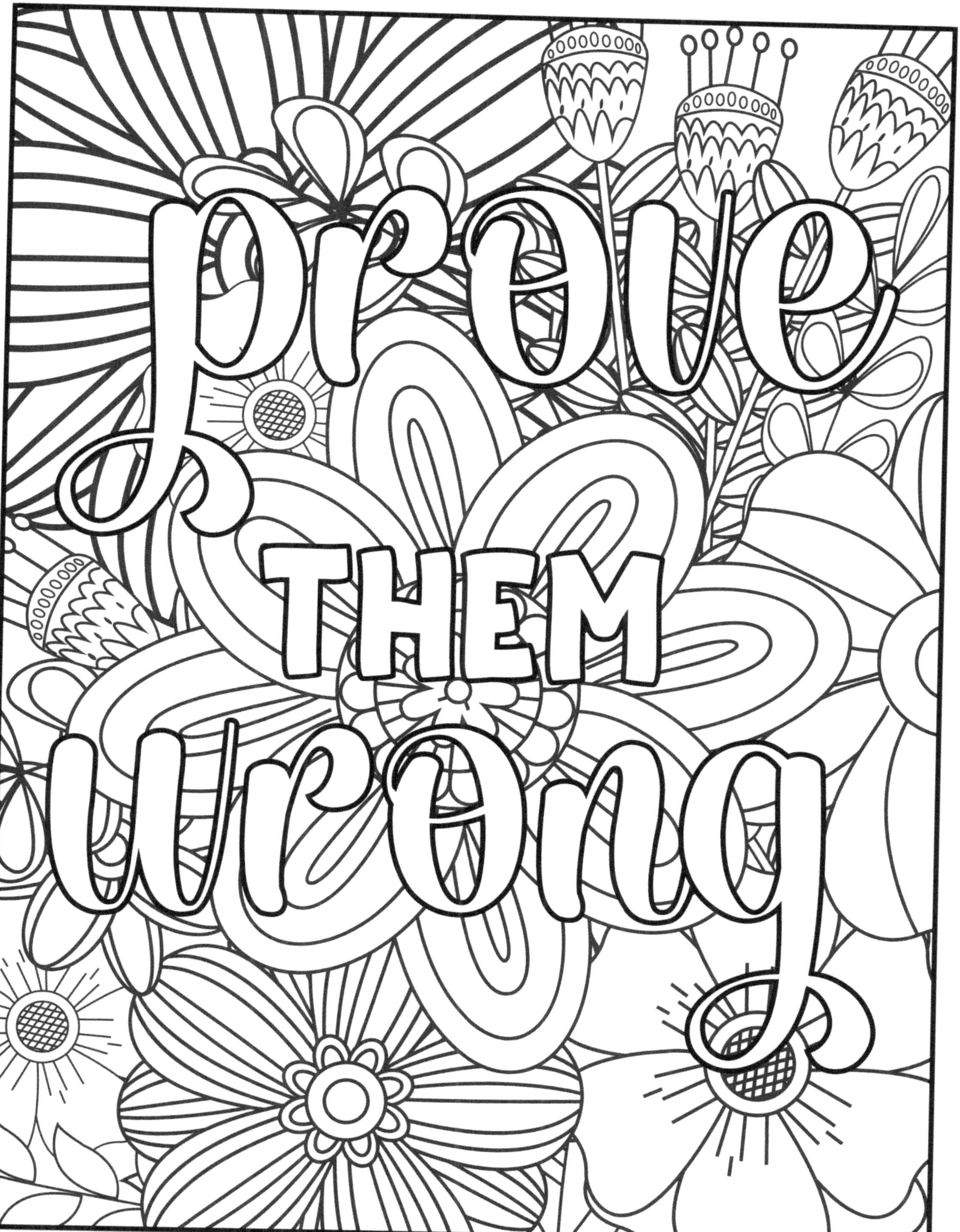
Prove
THEM
Wrong

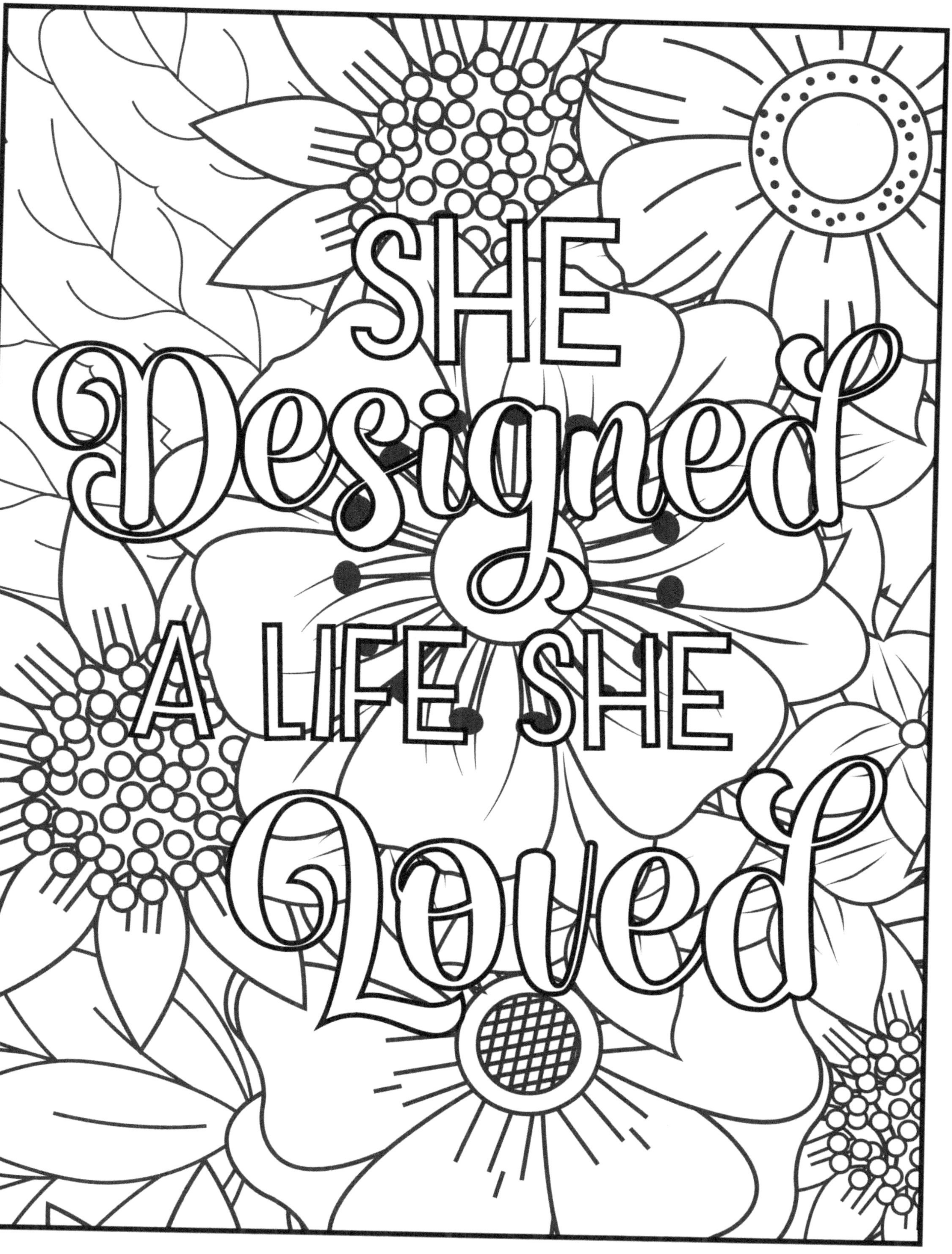
SHE
Designed
A LIFE SHE
Loved

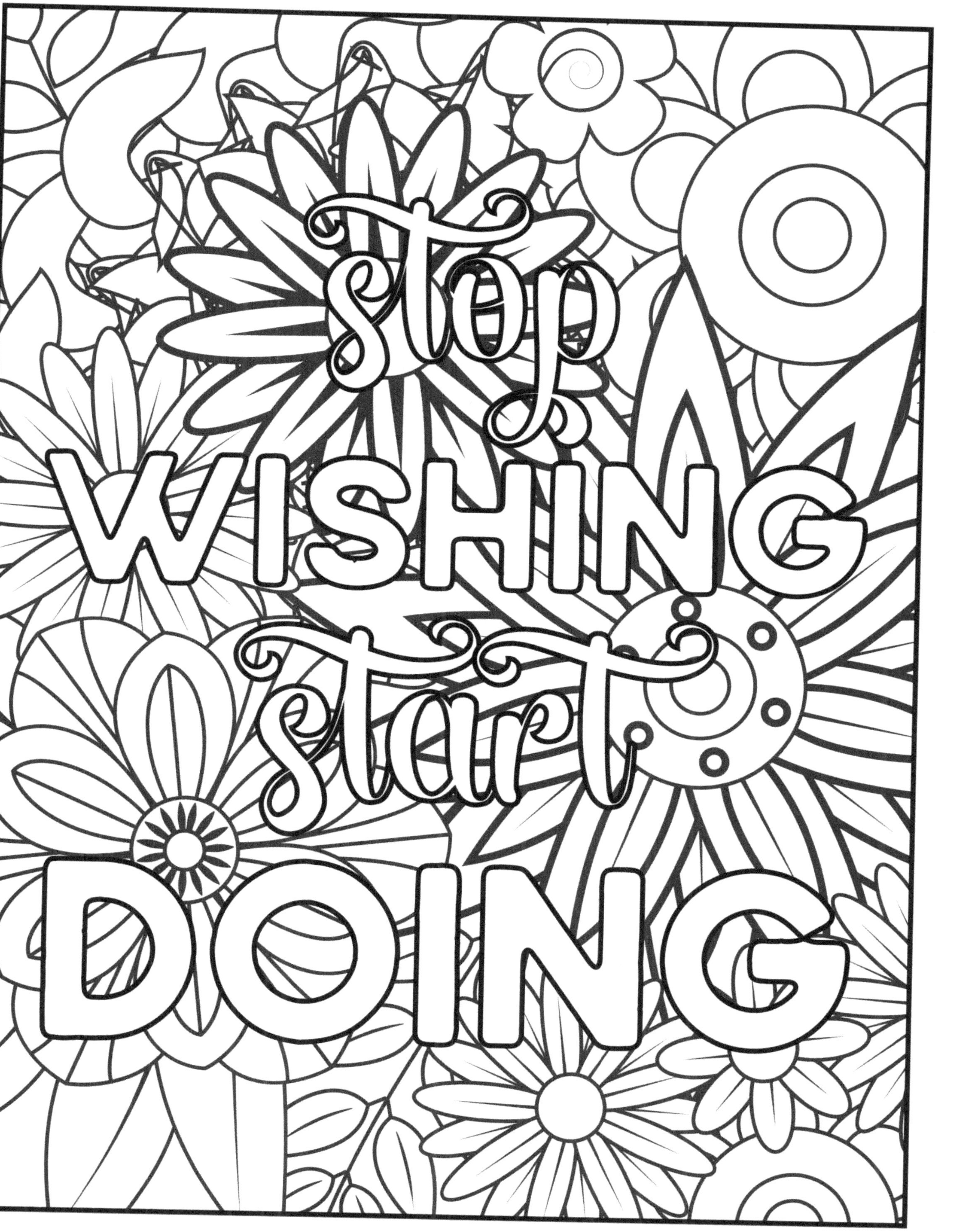
Stop
WISHING
start
DOING

www.ingramcontent.com/pod-product-compliance
Lightning Source LLC
Chambersburg PA
CBHW062206220526
45470CB00009B/2945
9798326392541